OXFORD BOOKWORMS LIBRARY

Crime and Mystery

Poisonous
Who can you trust?

ANN GIANOLA

Level 3 (1000 headwords)

Illustrated by Dylan Gibson

Series Editor: Rachel Bladon
Editor: Emma Wilkinson

OXFORD
UNIVERSITY PRESS

Great Clarendon Street, Oxford, OX2 6DP, United Kingdom

Oxford University Press is a department of the University of Oxford.
It furthers the University's objective of excellence in research, scholarship,
and education by publishing worldwide. Oxford is a registered trade
mark of Oxford University Press in the UK and in certain other countries

This edition © Oxford University Press 2023

The moral rights of the author have been asserted

First published in Oxford Bookworms 2023

10 9 8 7 6 5 4

ISBN: 978 0 19 426717 5   Book
ISBN: 978 0 19 426714 4   Book and audio pack

For more information on the Oxford Bookworms Library,
visit www.oup.com/elt/gradedreaders

ACKNOWLEDGEMENTS

Cover Images by: Getty Images (Dmitry_Tsvetkov) and Shutterstock (YIUCHEUNG)

Illustrations by: Dylan Gibson

*The publisher would like to thank the following for their permission to reproduce
photographs*: Shutterstock (Rawpixel.com)

CONTENTS

PEOPLE IN THIS STORY

Liza   a new student at Pinewood Academy

Suki   who becomes Liza's friend on her first day at the new school

Marco   also friends with Liza since her first day

Alex   who becomes Liza's boyfriend

Jade   a rich student from Pinewood Academy

Veda   a clever, successful student

Yang   a Pinewood student and computer genius

Aunt Evelyn   who looks after Liza

Inspector Leon   a police officer

Gina   Liza's lawyer in the police station

CHAPTER 1
'Hope u like prison'

03.12

Liza looked around the cold, empty room. One of the police officers had given her a blanket and she pulled it around her shoulders, but it did not stop her shaking. She was still wearing the beautiful, red dress and expensive shoes that she'd had on all evening. How had this happened? It had started as the best night of her life – the most fun that she'd ever had as a student at Pinewood Academy. She had been so happy; Alex had danced close to her all night, his hand on her back, his mouth near her ear.

Alex had danced close to Liza all night.

Now, Liza sat on a metal chair under a bright light. Inspector Leon, a man with thick, white hair and deep lines in his face, sat across from her. He looked at Liza's phone, which lay in a clear bag on the table. 'We've seen the messages. You've got some real problems, haven't you? But the bigger problem is the poison that we found in your bag. Do you know how it got there – or in Alex's drink?'

Liza just wanted to wake up from this terrible dream. It had felt unreal when Alex collapsed on the dance floor. At first, she'd thought that he was just trying to be funny, but then blood had come out of his mouth – and she had started to scream. Although Alex had been alive when they'd put him in the ambulance, he'd already looked like a ghost.

It had felt unreal when Alex collapsed on the dance floor.

Where was he now? Was he even alive? Tears fell from Liza's eyes. At only seventeen years old, what kind of future was there for either of them now?

'I don't know how the poison got into my bag, Inspector. But I didn't hurt Alex. I love Alex! And everything that I've told you is true!'

Inspector Leon looked at Liza carefully. Then he began asking her about the messages on her phone – the strange ones. She told him that, at first, there had been just a few. But recently, there had been more. No, she didn't know who'd sent them. Yes, she'd tried to block the sender. But they'd continued, and they'd come from a different number every time.

'So the last one came just a day or two ago?' asked Inspector Leon.

'Yes,' said Liza. It had been Thursday after school. As she'd pulled the phone from her pocket, she'd hoped it was a message from Alex. But it was another of the frightening ones. Who was sending them? 'Hope u like prison,' it had read. 'U won't look so pretty in the uniform.'

At lunch the next day, Liza had shown it to her friends, Marco and Suki.

'Oh, no,' said Suki, shaking her head slowly. 'They're getting worse.'

'I don't agree,' said Marco. 'The last one was: "You're going to die in prison". So, this one is nicer. And look, they think you're pretty, Liza! So, that's sweet, isn't it?' Marco was trying to make Liza laugh, but this wasn't funny. 'Don't worry,' he said, putting a hand on her shoulder. 'This is stupid. Someone is playing a game with you. They can't be serious.'

The inspector looked at his notes. 'How long have you been getting these?'

'For about three months,' Liza replied.

'Did you tell your parents or your teachers at Pinewood?' Liza had to tell him that she hadn't. But there were reasons for this. For a moment, Liza looked at herself in the two-way mirror on the wall. Behind it, she knew that other police officers were watching and listening.

'My mum is dead and I don't know my dad,' she said. 'I live with my aunt. She's great, but she's always busy. She's a nurse and works long hours, and I just didn't want to worry her.'

Liza looked at herself in the two-way mirror on the wall.

'And what about your teachers?' the inspector continued. 'Why didn't you talk to them?'

'Because I can't be a problem,' answered Liza, quietly blowing her nose. 'I'm one of the students... without money. I go to Pinewood on a scholarship, so I can't get into any trouble. It's a great school and I have – had – plans to go to a good university from there.'

Most of the time, Liza knew how to manage difficult people. It wasn't always easy and of course some students were always saying hurtful things about other people's hair, clothes, or the shape of their bodies. Last year, some girls had seen her boarding the number 8 bus for Eastside. They'd laughed aloud as they boarded a bus to a more expensive part of town. The next day, they'd called loudly, 'Don't be late for your bus. Your neighbours in Eastside will miss you.' Everyone had turned around to look at her, but Liza had pretended not to care.

Happily, Liza had made some real friends at Pinewood. Marco and Suki were lovely, and they were scholarship students like her. Recently, she'd become closer to a few kids who weren't on scholarships: Jade, Yang, Veda, and Alex. Alex. Everything that had happened with Alex still felt like a dream – or had felt like a dream, until that night. And now, he was lying in a hospital somewhere, and Liza didn't even know how he was.

She put her face in her hands and began to cry. Then she heard a noise from her phone, which was still in the bag on the table. Inspector Leon immediately opened it to see the message. This time it was a GIF of someone laughing.

Liza looked up as he read out the message. '"You're in big trouble now, Liza." What's this about?' he asked, shaking his head. 'And who sends things like that when a boy is lying ill in hospital?'

'I don't know!' cried Liza. 'I only know that someone poisoned Alex and they want everyone to think that it was me! I don't know why this person wants to hurt me... or us. But I didn't do it! I didn't put anything in Alex's drink, I promise!'

The inspector looked carefully at Liza for a moment. Then, he turned around towards the two-way mirror. Liza wondered what the inspector – and the other officers – thought. Did they really think she was a murderer, trying to save her own skin?

CHAPTER 2
Beautiful in red

`04.06`

Inspector Leon pushed Liza's phone to the other side of the table. 'Tell me what happened yesterday. What did you do before the dance?'

'Well,' answered Liza quietly. 'Marco and I got ready at my friend Jade's house. She let me borrow this dress.'

Liza looked down at Jade's dress, which was now covered with Alex's blood. Cleaning the dress was the least of her problems at this moment, but it looked terrible. When she'd put it on, before the dance, Liza had felt like a movie star.

'That's it!' Jade had cried, as Liza stood in front of a big mirror. 'That's the one that you're wearing to the dance tonight. And I have *everything* to go with it,' she added, and she'd disappeared into a dressing room, where she kept her clothes, shoes, gloves, and bags. It seemed almost as large as Liza's flat.

'Girl,' Marco said, looking at Liza and smiling, 'you're so beautiful! I want to marry you now! Well, that's not true actually – I secretly want to marry your boyfriend, Alex.'

'That's no secret,' Jade laughed, throwing some expensive, red shoes and a small bag onto a chair next to Liza. 'But you know Alex likes the ladies. Sorry about that, Marco.' Then she took a long look at Liza. 'But you're right about one thing: Liza is *very* beautiful. And Alex will love her even more in that dress.'

That afternoon at Jade's house had been wonderful. After lunch, some people had arrived to do their hair and make-up. Marco had smiled as Jade introduced Sara and Juan. 'I've never been so happy,' he whispered to Liza. He immediately introduced himself to Juan. 'Juan, my love,' he said, shaking his hand. 'I'd love a smokey-eye for tonight. Can you please do that for me?'

'A smokey-eye!' laughed Liza. 'What is that?'

'Liza, where have you been living all this time?' said Marco. 'Dark make-up on the top and bottom of the eye. It looks fabulous!'

Liza smiled as she remembered that moment.

'Is something funny?' asked the inspector. 'Let's not forget that we're talking about a possible murder.'

'I haven't forgotten,' said Liza. 'Sorry.'

'So, what happened next?' he asked.

'Well,' said Liza, closing her eyes, 'Veda, another kid from Pinewood, came over later. And Alex met us at Jade's in the early evening – at around seven o'clock. Then we all picked up our coats and got into the limo. Marco and I had never ridden in a limo before, so that was very exciting.'

'To be clear,' said the inspector, 'five people were in the limo: Alex, Jade, Marco, Veda, and you.'

'Yes,' answered Liza. Of course, Liza had wanted Suki to join them, but she'd refused.

'I don't live in their world,' Suki had said on the phone earlier that morning. 'I won't pretend to have money when I don't. And big, black cars make me think of dead bodies. I don't travel that way.'

Marco and Liza had never ridden in a limo before.

But perhaps there was another reason: Suki didn't like Liza and Alex being together. She had never thought that Alex was good enough for her best friend. Liza knew that Suki cared about her, but why did she have to be so moody all the time?

'OK, so you went in the limo and everyone arrived at the dance. Then what?' asked the inspector.

'Well… Alex and I danced most of the night,' answered Liza, opening her eyes and looking straight at the inspector. 'All night, really. I mean, we sat down and had a drink sometimes, but the rest of the time we were dancing. Until midnight.'

'That's when Alex collapsed on the dance floor,' said Inspector Leon.

'Yes,' said Liza. 'It was awful,' she added, new tears appearing in her eyes. 'He was in so much pain!'

Liza remembered how the paramedics had run to try to help Alex while the police moved everyone to one side of the room and began searching them. She had almost not noticed the police checking their bags and everyone's pockets because she could not stop thinking about Alex.

Then, suddenly, an officer had pulled a small bottle out of her bag. Immediately, he'd pushed everyone back and put the bottle into a clear bag, calling more officers for help. 'That isn't mine!' Liza had cried. 'And I have no idea how it got in my bag!'

For a moment, Liza sat quietly across from the inspector. She couldn't describe how she'd felt at the dance, with everyone staring at her and shaking their heads. Then she'd

An officer had pulled a small bottle out of Liza's bag.

had to watch as they'd carried Alex out. He'd arrived at the dance in a limo, and he was leaving in an ambulance.

'So, you say that you'd never seen the bottle of poison which was found in your bag?' the inspector went on.

'No, never!' cried Liza.

'Are you sure it wasn't there already when this friend Jade lent it to you?'

'No, the bag was empty. I know it was.'

'Was the bag with you all evening?'

'Well, no, not when I was dancing,' said Liza. 'I left it at our table.'

'And who was sitting at your table?'

'All our friends were there,' said Liza. 'Marco, Suki, Jade,

Veda, and Yang.'

'Liza,' said the inspector, 'did any of your friends have a reason for wanting to hurt Alex – or you?'

'No!' said Liza. She thought about her friends. Marco and Suki had always loved her. And although Jade was from a very different world, she had helped Liza a lot – and become a close friend. Jade had also liked Liza and Alex being together: 'It's Al-iza!' she always cried when she saw them, putting their names together. 'I'm just so happy that you two are a thing now!'

Liza knew that Veda liked her, too. Yes, they'd competed against each other in school. And when Liza had won the big science award, Veda had been hurt. But that was weeks ago. They'd had fun together at Jade's house before the dance, too. Yang was another good friend at Pinewood. He wasn't as popular as the others, but he was very sweet. He never started trouble – in fact, he usually found answers to problems.

There were some great kids at Pinewood Academy. They must know that she hadn't poisoned Alex. But perhaps the inspector was right. Did one of them know who had… ?

CHAPTER 3
Pinewood

`05.33`

A police officer brought Liza a sandwich and a glass of water while the inspector got another cup of coffee. 'I think we need to start at the beginning, Liza,' he said. 'You arrived at Pinewood Academy in September, didn't you? Tell me about being on a scholarship. It made you different from the other kids… the ones with money, didn't it?'

'You don't have to answer that,' said Liza's lawyer, Gina, a tall woman with red hair. She'd recently arrived and sat next to Liza.

'Thank you, but I want to answer his questions,' Liza replied. 'I have nothing to hide. So, yes,' she continued, turning to the inspector. 'I started there on a scholarship. Most of the kids at Pinewood go to good universities. And I wanted to do that, too.'

Liza bit into her sandwich and thought about her first day at school. That was when she'd met Marco and Suki. It cost most kids a lot of money to go to Pinewood, but Liza, Marco, and Suki went for free. So, they were different from the others. They weren't born rich. They didn't drive big, new cars. And they didn't live in the expensive parts of town. But Pinewood Academy accepted a few students like them every year, so Liza and her friends had felt very lucky.

Many students knew who the ones with scholarships were, and sometimes that made things difficult. Liza, Marco, and Suki sometimes heard other kids say that scholarships were unfair – their parents had worked hard to pay the full price and send their kids to Pinewood, so why did others go there free? Those kids did not understand how lucky they were.

Marco always replied to these questions easily because he knew how to make people laugh. 'Pinewood chose me because I'm handsome and wonderful,' he explained to one boy who tried to argue with him about money. 'Clearly, Pinewood chose you for other reasons.' Marco was just being funny, of course. But he was able to close down the conversation.

Suki didn't talk to the other people at school very much. 'Pinewood is fine,' she always said to Liza and Marco, 'but most of the people here are awful. I don't need any more friends – just you two.' Liza loved Marco and Suki, but she'd also been happy to make more friends.

First, she'd met Veda in the science laboratory. Liza had bought a new coat a few days earlier, and Veda had come in wearing the same coat, so they'd laughed about being 'coat sisters'. Veda was clever and interesting, and her parents were successful scientists. Yes, she'd told Liza many times that her parents had built the science lab at the university and that their names were on a building at the hospital. But Veda was right to be proud of them, wasn't she?

Next, Liza had become friends with Yang. He was the star in computer science lessons, the one who often knew more than their teacher. Although Yang was very nice and helpful, Liza only wanted to be his friend – and nothing more. She'd had to make that clear when he'd reached for her hand one day after school. 'I'm not looking for anything like that,' she'd said, pulling her hand away. 'I hope you can understand.'

Later, Liza had met Jade and Alex. At first, she'd thought they were together. They seemed like people who had been girlfriend and boyfriend for a long time. Jade always had her arm around Alex, and he always looked very comfortable with her. 'Well, that's true love,' Liza had thought. 'Will I ever feel that way about another person?'

But Liza had been wrong about Jade and Alex. She'd seen them walking out of school one day and, for some reason, she'd decided to talk to them. 'So, how long have you two been together?' she'd asked. Alex had laughed loudly.

Jade always had her arm around Alex.

'Together? Jade and me?' he cried. 'OK, that's the craziest thing that I've heard all day!'

'Yes, that is so crazy,' Jade agreed, smiling, but not laughing. 'We're just really good friends, aren't we, Alex?' she said, gently brushing his face with her hand. 'We've known each other since we were babies; our parents work together.'

'Think of us as brother and sister,' Alex said, looking at Liza with his kind, brown eyes. 'How about you? Do you have a boyfriend?' Liza felt her face turn red.

'Stop, Alex!' Jade cried. 'Don't make this poor girl uncomfortable.' Then she put her hand on Liza's shoulder and let it stay there for a while. 'You've probably got to catch your bus,' she said. 'I hear that it takes a long time to get to Eastside.'

'It's quicker than you think,' Suki said, walking towards them. Then she brushed Jade's hand off Liza. 'I'm sure that you spend much more time in front of a mirror. And next time you're looking in one, please ask yourself why you think you're better than other people – when you're not.'

Neither Jade nor Alex said a word. After an uncomfortable silence, Suki pulled Liza's arm and they walked away. But Liza turned around and smiled at Alex. And he smiled back, pushing the thick, black hair out of his dark eyes. Alex had clearly found the moment amusing. 'What was that about, Suki?' Liza asked. 'We were just talking.'

'You're very intelligent, Liza,' Suki answered, 'but you can be wrong about some people. I've seen and heard Jade around school. She isn't nice. She's mean and she only cares about herself. And Alex is nothing special. In fact, he's a big flirt. Neither one of them is worth your time.'

'Suki,' Liza said, laughing. 'I'm a big girl – I can take care of myself. No one is as important to me as you and Marco, but it's OK if I talk to other people, too. The Pinewood kids aren't all bad. Some are very nice,' she said, turning around once again and looking at Alex. 'Really nice, to be honest.'

So, looking back, this was quite a good time for Liza. She was doing well at Pinewood, and she'd made more friends. And now Alex – tall and handsome, with that beautiful smile – had begun to talk to her.

But something changed around then, too. In the last month, she'd had several anonymous messages from someone who clearly liked her – heart emojis and messages that said 'u r beautiful' and things like that. Although she didn't like getting messages from someone that she didn't know, they hadn't felt worrying. But the next anonymous message that came through on her phone was different.

CHAPTER 4

The award

`06.19`

'Stay in your lane,' said Liza aloud, remembering the message.

'What did you say?' asked Gina, putting her pen on the table. Liza had closed her eyes and fallen asleep for a few seconds.

'Sorry,' replied Liza. 'I was dreaming about the anonymous message that I got, just after I first began talking to Alex. Someone sent a message that said, "stay in your lane".'

'Yes,' said Inspector Leon. 'I saw that one. But what do you think it meant? Was it about you and Alex?' He took a drink of his coffee.

'Possibly,' answered Liza. 'Perhaps it was telling me that Alex was too good for me, and I needed to stay in my place and find a boyfriend in Eastside... or... I don't know what.'

At the time, Liza hadn't fully understood the message. Many things were happening in her life. Just two weeks after the first conversation with Alex and Jade, she had won an important science competition. The award had come with money – and an invitation to study at a summer school at Oxford University. Liza had been so happy, and her Aunt Evelyn had proudly told everyone in their building.

The news about Liza winning had travelled quickly. Teachers and students at Pinewood stopped to talk to her and shake her hand. 'Well done, Liza!' Mr Patel, her science teacher, said. 'You're a great example to the other students.'

After school, on the day when the award came through,

Liza and her friends had sat talking in a small group under a tree.

'I love this for you, Liza!' Marco said excitedly. 'This year, Oxford; next year, the world! So, because you're going to be rich and famous now, can I borrow some money?'

But among all her friends, Alex was the happiest for Liza. 'Liza has everything!' he said, putting his strong arm around her – and keeping it there. 'She's intelligent. She's beautiful. And now, she's an award-winning scientist – a real genius! Everyone, you're looking at the most successful student at Pinewood Academy.'

At that moment, Liza's life had felt wonderful. She had a place at a summer school at Oxford. And Alex – the boy who she'd quietly begun liking – clearly liked her, too.

'Thanks,' said Liza, enjoying the warm feeling of his arm across her back.

'He's right,' said Yang, joining their circle. He stared uncomfortably at Alex's arm around Liza. 'Your work was awesome.' But Yang looked a little sad as he said it. 'I mean, it's hard, I won't lie… because I… the rest of us… lost, but… good job, Liza.'

'You all did great, too!' said Liza. 'Really, this is a surprise. I didn't think that I would… '

'Neither did I,' said Veda, appearing suddenly. 'I honestly didn't think you had a chance.'

'What an awful thing to say!' cried Jade, looking at Veda crossly. 'You should be ashamed of yourself, Veda. Liza won. You lost. Just accept it!'

'Oh, I didn't mean it,' said Veda, pushing Liza playfully.

'You should be ashamed of yourself, Veda,' said Jade.

'We're just having a laugh here, aren't we?'

Liza wasn't surprised that Veda was upset. All her life, Veda had gone to the best schools. How had a girl from Eastside stolen this award from her? Winning second place had just made Veda angrier because she was so close to first. And there was Liza, in Alex's arms, saying that the others 'all did great, too'. So, perhaps it was Veda who had told Liza to stay in her lane. If she had, Liza now understood why.

But at the time, her head had been too full of other things – exciting things – to worry about how Veda was feeling.

For a minute, she closed her eyes and remembered that day, just a few days after the award, when Alex had walked with her to the bus stop. Just as the number 8 had arrived, he had kissed her lips. And Liza had never felt so happy.

Alex and Liza being together was big news at school, although several kids weren't pleased about it. Marco had put out his bottom lip and said, 'I love you, Liza. But I also hate you. Alex was mine and you've broken my heart!' Once again, she knew – or thought – that Marco was saying it for a laugh. But it had been a strange time. Before, Liza hadn't been anyone special at Pinewood. Now, she'd become a big story.

'People know you now,' Yang had said, sitting down next to Liza in the computer lab. 'I heard three girls whispering about you at lunch – and not in a good way. What do you think about that?'

'I don't like it,' said Liza, shaking her head. 'I mean, I enjoyed winning the science award. That made me happy, of course. But I don't enjoy people talking about me because of Alex. That's just… not fair,' she added, pushing her long, brown hair off her face.

'Perhaps they're surprised, you know,' Yang said, 'because they thought you weren't looking for anything like that.'

'I'm sorry, Yang,' Liza answered, as she remembered the day when he'd tried to take her hand. 'But, well, people don't know anything about me. And I can't stop liking the person who I like,' she added, putting her hand into her pocket.

'Or perhaps it's because you and Alex are very different,' Yang explained, looking at Liza's pretty face. 'It's the old story: the rich kid likes the poor girl from the wrong side of town. People think you and Alex don't fit together – they don't understand it.'

'Stop,' Liza said, looking at Yang angrily. 'I don't care how much money Alex has, and he doesn't care where I live.'

'Or perhaps it just upsets people,' Yang continued, 'because they're very jealous. If they can't have you, then nobody can. For some people, I guess, it's a thin line between love and hate. You know… '

'No, Yang, I don't know,' Liza cried, her voice getting louder. 'It's frightening that people can think that way.'

Then Liza and Yang had turned to their computers.

'Don't forget. It's my life,' Liza said. 'And if the girls at lunch – and all the other kids here – want to talk about me, then they should just… just… stay in their lane!'

'Don't forget. It's my life,' Liza said.

CHAPTER 5
More messages

`06.42`

'The first messages weren't too bad,' said Liza, as Inspector Leon and Gina wrote notes. 'Later, they got much worse.'

'I can see that,' replied the inspector, looking at the sheets of paper in front of him.

Now Liza was drinking coffee, too. She had to stay awake and tell the inspector and her lawyer everything that she knew. They needed her help to arrest the real criminal – the one who had tried to kill Alex.

'So, the messages from February, when you were getting to know Alex, hadn't frightened you,' said the inspector.

'Not really,' answered Liza. 'But I didn't like getting them. If you have something to say, you should say it to a person's face. There was the "stay in your lane" message, like I said, but most of the first ones were just stupid: "u don't even know him", or "this isn't real love", with a few broken heart emojis and tearful faces.'

At the time, Liza had thought about the girls – the ones that Yang had told her about – whispering her name at lunch. Perhaps they had sat in front of their phones, laughing, as they'd written the next message: 'he isn't right for you'.

'They're not wrong,' Suki had said, when that message had arrived and she'd read it over Liza's shoulder. 'He isn't right for you. Perhaps you should listen to them.'

'Stop, Suki!' Liza had cried. 'Please don't agree with the people who are doing this!'

Suki took Liza's hand and smiled. 'OK, I'm sorry,' she said. 'And I'm sure it isn't fun to get all this rubbish on your phone… but it is strange to see you and Alex together. I didn't think you'd fall in love with a rich, Pinewood boy – a person who doesn't have to work for a thing and just goes into business with Mummy and Daddy. I thought that you'd like someone more interesting.'

'I don't really care what you think,' Liza said, crossing her arms. 'I've fallen for Alex. And I've fallen hard. We're like Romeo and Juliet.'

'You know it didn't end well for those two,' Suki said. 'Remember, Romeo drank poison and Juliet killed herself. Is that really how you want your story to go?'

Liza had to laugh at that. 'No, I want the Romeo and Juliet story that ends with happily ever after.'

At that moment, Alex had walked across the grass to join them. 'Hey, Babe,' he said to Liza, putting his arms around her. 'And, hi, Suki,' he added. 'How's it going?'

'Hello, Romeo,' said Suki, picking up her bag. 'You should stay away from poison, you know. Juliet here likes having you around.' She turned and walked away from them.

'What is she talking about?' Alex asked. 'Why doesn't your friend like me?'

'Well, I like you,' Marco said, joining them. 'Although I'm not sure about your girlfriend any more, because she stole you from me,' he added, making a pretend-angry face at Liza. Both Alex and Liza laughed.

'Don't be sad, Marco,' Alex said, smiling. 'There are lots of other fish in the sea.'

'*Juliet here likes having you around,*' *said Suki.*

'I know there are,' said Marco, looking around at the other students outside. 'You see, I've forgotten you already.'

'Forgotten who?' Jade asked, joining their circle.

'Forgotten me,' Alex answered. 'Oh, it's nothing. We were just… '

'Girl! You look beautiful today!' Marco cried, moving closer to Jade and studying her make-up. 'This was the work of a… genius!'

'It was! I have someone – Juan – who comes to my place when I want to feel special,' Jade replied.

'Make-up works like medicine, doesn't it?' Marco said. 'You look fabulous! You must feel good now.'

'I do, thank you,' Jade replied, blowing a kiss at Marco. She looked at Liza, who had both her arms around Alex. 'How is Al-iza? You two look so in love. It's sweet, really! I think… I'm going… to cry!'

Marco noticed the real tears in Jade's eyes.

'Don't!' he screamed. 'You'll destroy your make-up! Then poor Juan will have to do it again!'

`07.08`

At the police station, Liza continued to answer questions. Then, while Gina left the room to take a phone call, Inspector Leon wrote more notes. For a minute, Liza closed her eyes and remembered those first few weeks of her and Alex being together. Like make-up was for Jade, Alex had been a kind of medicine for Liza. He was her Romeo. But when Romeo died from taking poison, what happened to Juliet?

Liza opened her eyes and looked down again at her red dress. It felt so wrong to wear it in a place like this, and she wished she had some jeans and a warm top – something comfortable, something from the real world.

'So,' said the inspector, 'these messages. They suddenly changed, didn't they, at the beginning of March? A week or two after you and Alex had got together?'

'Yes,' replied Liza. 'That's when the messages became different. And they weren't anonymous any more. Each one came from a different number.'

Liza remembered talking to Suki after the first one had arrived.

'How can someone write things like this?' she'd asked. 'Seriously, this makes me feel sick.'

'Really? What does it say?' Suki asked, moving closer to Liza.

'I don't think you want to see it,' Liza said.

'It can't be that bad. Give me your phone,' Suki said, taking it from Liza's hand. '"Someone's going 2 die",' she read. She looked up at Liza, her eyes open wide in surprise. 'What kind of monster sends a message like this?'

'I don't know,' said Liza.

'There's a number. Have you called it?'

'Yes,' said Liza. 'But the line is dead. It doesn't ring.'

'That's strange,' said Suki. 'Liza, I really don't like this.'

CHAPTER 6
The spa

Liza had enjoyed having a boyfriend, but the messages had been a dark cloud in her life. When she showed them to Alex, he just told her not to worry. 'It's nothing, Liza!' he said. 'People have messaged me strange things before,' he added, kissing her gently. 'Forget the messages – and the stupid people who are sending them.'

Forgetting about the messages wasn't so easy for Liza. They frightened her. She blocked the sender every time, but then the next one came from a different number. She'd thought about changing her number. But when she talked about it with Yang one afternoon, he'd told her not to spend time and money on it. 'If they have your number now, they'll get it again. It's really difficult to contain information like that, when so many people know you.'

'But they're horrible, Yang! Look at these!' Liza had said, showing her phone to him after their lesson. 'This one came just last night: "ur death will be painful". Isn't it clear? Someone wants to kill me. I couldn't sleep half the night.'

Yang stared at Liza.

'What? I didn't know... that you were getting messages like this,' Yang said slowly. 'Last time we talked, you'd just had a few broken hearts and other stupid emojis. This is bad.' He ran his fingers through his untidy, black hair.

'Can you help me, Yang?' Liza asked. 'I mean, you know so much about this kind of thing – you're a computer genius. Can you find out who is sending these to me?'

'I'll try,' said Yang. 'Let me borrow your phone for the afternoon and I'll do what I can.'

But when Yang had given Liza her phone back later that afternoon, he was shaking his head. 'The messages are coming from burner phones,' he said. 'They're cheap phones that people throw away after they've used them, so we can't find out anything about them. I'm really sorry.'

'Why are you sorry?' Jade asked, appearing suddenly behind Yang. 'And how can you feel sorry for Liza? This girl is beautiful; she's got brains and she's in love. And you've only got the brains bit.'

Yang didn't answer. He turned and walked away. 'See you on Monday, Liza,' he said, waving. 'And try not to worry.'

'Liza,' said Jade, now walking next to her, 'I don't know what you're worried about. But I have the answer: tomorrow is Saturday, and you and I are going to a spa!'

'I can't do that, Jade,' said Liza, watching Yang disappear into the crowd of Pinewood students. 'That sounds very expensive, and I'm afraid I just don't have the money for… '

'But I do,' said Jade, putting her finger over Liza's lips. 'I'll pay for everything. Your only job is to relax and be happy.'

'I need that job, too,' said a voice behind them. It was Marco. 'I want to relax and be happy! Who's paying?'

Jade laughed hard. 'OK, Marco,' she said. 'I'll invite you, too because you're a funny boy – and you actually need a little help. Please don't be hurt by my honesty, but your skin is looking so tired.'

'I'm not hurt! I'm grateful!' Marco replied, with a big smile. 'I'm so excited to spend time with my favourite girls tomorrow. So, Jade… we'll meet where and when?'

'I'll decide and message you both later,' Jade answered. 'Is that OK?'

The next day, Liza and Marco had met Jade at an expensive spa on Park Avenue.

'Well, this is wonderful,' Marco said, as a young woman gave him a soft, pink robe.

'Thank you!' Liza said, taking one, too.

'The dressing rooms are on the left. Would you like any help?' the young woman asked.

'No, thank you,' said Liza. 'But thank you very much. I'll just go in there and put on my robe. And thank you so, so much!'

'Stop thanking people,' Jade said, in a voice that was loud enough for everyone to hear. 'I've paid a lot of money for this, so these people have to be nice to us. It's their job. Do you understand? We're at the top; they're at the bottom.'

'Well,' Liza said, her face turning red, 'they're people, just like you and me. And I want to thank them.'

Jade said nothing for a moment. Then she smiled and put her hand on Liza's shoulder. 'Oh Liza, you are funny sometimes,' she said. She waved her hand towards the dressing rooms. 'Go!' she said, pushing both Liza and Marco. 'Let's get ready. Our faces can't wait!'

Forty minutes later, Marco, Jade, and Liza were relaxing in a comfortable room, their faces covered in a beautiful-smelling skin product. They had pieces of cucumber on their eyes, too.

'Thank you!' Liza had said, accepting the green circles

gratefully. 'But I don't need vegetables on my eyes!' she'd whispered to Jade and Marco.

'Leave the cucumbers where they are,' said Jade. 'They're very important. You need them for the dark circles under your eyes, Liza. Recently, you've looked so tired. I've been worried about you!'

'Liza studies all night,' said Marco. 'The poor girl doesn't know when to turn off the lights and go to sleep.'

Marco was right. Liza had had a lot of very late nights recently. But she wasn't just studying. She was worrying about the messages and asking herself why someone wanted to hurt or possibly kill her.

'She needs to rest,' Jade said. 'She needs to stay pretty.

Marco, Jade, and Liza had pieces of cucumber on their eyes.

There are a hundred other kids at Pinewood who want to get their hands on Alex.' She took the piece of cucumber off one eye and looked at Liza. 'And several other girls are waiting to get him back. They know what Alex is like.'

'What are you talking about, Jade?' Liza asked, taking the cucumbers from her eyes. Marco did the same. The conversation was suddenly getting very interesting. As Marco listened, he started to eat one of his cucumbers.

'Oh, Liza,' Jade said, 'you aren't Alex's first love, and you won't be his last. At Pinewood,' she continued, putting the cucumber back on her eye, 'he's always been very popular with the ladies. I don't want to hurt you, but you must know that Alex has been – and always will be – a busy, busy boy.'

CHAPTER 7
'Who's Liza?'

Liza had felt a pain in her heart. For a full minute, she hadn't said a word. Then she'd got up. 'You know, I'm really tired,' she said. 'Thanks for this, Jade, but I think I should go… ' Immediately, Jade jumped up, her two cucumbers falling to the floor.

'No!' Jade shouted. 'You can't go, Liza! I'm so sorry! I shouldn't talk about Alex like that. You're his girlfriend now and honestly, I've never seen him so happy. Please stay longer. You'll feel like a new person.'

Liza stood for a moment, looking at Jade. Then she slowly sat back down. 'I'm sorry, too, Jade. I'm just getting upset very easily at the moment. There's a lot happening in my life. And of course, I know Alex has had a lot of girlfriends at Pinewood. I mean… he's Alex.'

'Girls, let's enjoy our day at the spa,' Marco said, eating his other cucumber. 'We all came here to relax, didn't we?'

In the late afternoon, Jade, Liza, and Marco had left the spa. As they came outside, everyone felt happier. But Liza was worrying about the cost of the day for Jade, and she opened her bag. 'Let me pay a bit for today,' she said, taking out her phone. 'I'll send you some… '

'No, you won't!' Jade cried, taking Liza's phone from her and putting it back in her bag. 'I was happy to do it for you… and for Marco.'

'Liza, you heard Jade,' Marco said, his phone deep in his pocket. 'She's very kindly refused, so please – let's stop talking about money.'

Liza felt bad about being upset earlier. Yes, Jade sometimes said things that seemed unkind – and she wasn't always polite to people. But at the spa, perhaps Liza had been a good example to her. She'd actually heard Jade say thank you to the people at the spa when they left. So, Jade had listened to Liza.

Jade's words about Alex's other girlfriends had still been mean – and they had cut Liza like a knife. Was Liza just one more girl in a long line of others? Jade had known Alex for many years, so Liza couldn't argue with the facts. But she knew that she mustn't be jealous of Alex's past. Jealousy was a terrible thing. It was called the 'green-eyed monster' for a reason. It destroyed people.

As Liza, Marco, and Jade walked away from the spa, Suki, Veda, and Yang suddenly appeared. It was very unusual for Suki to spend time with people from Pinewood out of school, and Liza stared at her.

'This is a surprise,' Liza said. 'I didn't know that you three were friends.'

'Well, I'm more surprised! Are you actually going to spas now?' Suki laughed. 'It doesn't surprise me about you, Marco, but, Liza, you've really changed! What's next? Are you going to get a new nose?'

'Be nice, Suki,' said Jade, shaking her head, 'and perhaps I'll invite you to the spa next time. Just look at Marco now,' she added. 'Isn't he beautiful?'

'I don't go to spas,' Suki said. 'They're for rich people – or people who pretend to be rich.'

'Are you actually going to spas now?' Suki laughed.

'But they're so much fun!' Veda said. 'My mum took me here for my last birthday, and we had a great time. Now, I'm too busy with school,' she continued, looking at Liza. 'But if you marry Alex, then you don't need to study. You'll only need to plan parties – and look pretty. Isn't that the job that you're really looking for? I mean, forget about that summer school. It's much more important – for you – to go to the spa.'

'You're still angry about Liza winning the science award, aren't you?' Jade said. 'I can smell your jealousy from here. Sorry, Veda, but you can't compete with a genius.'

'Stop... all of you!' Yang cried. 'Isn't life hard enough without... ?'

'We're just having a laugh,' said Suki, gently pushing Yang. 'You're always so serious! Liza and Marco are my oldest friends at Pinewood. And friends do this to each other, don't they? Honestly, I hope you had a fun day. And Marco,' she added, 'you do look good!'

08.13

At the police station, Liza went into the bathroom. A woman police officer watched as she washed her face and hands. When Liza felt the cold water on her skin, she remembered what had happened after she'd left the spa. Of course, she'd really wanted to talk to Alex. But that day, he'd gone with his parents to a business lunch at a hotel. 'It's not a big thing,' he'd explained, 'but I have to go. It's important for the family to appear at these things. We eat lunch and shake hands with people. It's part of the game,' he'd added, smiling. 'Sorry we can't get together after the spa. Have fun with Jade and Marco – and don't forget to relax!'

As she'd walked home from the spa, Liza had begun thinking about what Jade had said about Alex, and she'd felt very worried again. She didn't want to be a jealous girlfriend who was always checking on her boyfriend when she wasn't with him, and she knew that she needed to trust Alex. But she really wanted to talk to him. Liza tried to message him, but he didn't reply. She waited for a bit, then messaged him a second time. And again, he didn't answer. Finally, Liza decided to call, and her heart was beating loudly as the phone rang. It rang four times before she heard Alex's voice.

'Hello, Liza!' he said. 'I'm still at this… thing with my parents. Can I call you back?'

'Sure!' said Liza. Then she heard a girl laughing.

'Who's Liza?' the girl asked, laughing harder. 'And why do you need to call her back?'

'I'll explain later,' Alex said, and he sounded different, Liza thought. Also, was Alex actually speaking to her – or to the other girl? She felt sick.

'All right,' said Liza. 'Sorry. Yes, we can talk later. Or tomorrow.'

Without another word, Alex ended the call. Liza had tried to fight back the tears in her eyes. Then three messages had appeared on her phone: 'hate u', 'alex mine', and 'just die'.

CHAPTER 8
A phone call

`08.43`

'It sounds like many of the messages that you got were telling you that Alex was spending some of his time with other girls,' said Inspector Leon.

'Yes,' said Liza. 'Clearly the person who was sending them wanted me to think that.'

'And what did Alex say about all of this?' asked the inspector.

'He just said that none of the things in the messages were true,' said Liza. 'He told me to trust him. Then Alex began getting strange messages, too. But the ones he got were very different to mine: flirty messages and photos of pretty girls. They were sent anonymously. He thought they were just funny, but they made me really upset. So, about a week ago, we argued about them after school. I asked him why he was getting those messages, and I said I… ' Liza's voice shook a little as she remembered. 'I said I didn't believe him. I thought he knew who was sending them. I told him what Jade had said at the spa – that he was a busy, busy boy. We were talking loudly, and several people heard us.'

'And then?' asked the inspector.

'I left school in tears, and ran towards the bus stop. But Alex followed me. And this time we talked – we really talked – about everything,' said Liza.

Liza left school in tears, and ran towards the bus stop.

'What did he say?' asked the inspector.

'He said a lot of things… that just made me believe him. He said it was true that he'd had a lot of girlfriends, but he said I was… different. I told him about the phone call after the spa, too, and he explained that the girl that I'd heard was his sister. She's fourteen, and she was trying to find out about me all day, he said.'

The inspector wrote some more notes. 'Let's talk a bit more about your friends now, Liza,' he said. 'Did any of them have a reason for wanting to make trouble for you and Alex? You said that Suki, for example, didn't like you and Alex being together. And Veda,' he continued, looking at his notes, 'was angry when you won the big science award. And Yang… he'd liked you before you were with Alex, right? But you hadn't liked him? And Jade? She seemed nice… but she was always very interested in your love life, wasn't she? And there was one more person… '

'You're thinking of Marco,' said Liza. 'And believe me, Marco did not poison Alex. None of my friends did! They're not criminals!'

At that moment, a police officer entered the room and told the inspector that there was an important phone call for him. The officer stayed in the room with Liza and Gina. Liza closed her eyes.

'Don't worry, Liza. We'll have some answers soon,' Gina said kindly. But Liza didn't want to talk about it any more. She knew that none of her friends had done this – poisoned her boyfriend and sent those horrible messages. It had to be another person – or a group of people. Pinewood was a big school. Perhaps it was one of the girls who Yang had heard whispering about her at lunch. Perhaps the messages had started as a funny game and then things had gone too far.

At that moment, the inspector returned to the room. 'So, I have some news,' he said. 'Your friend Marco is in the hospital right now. He was poisoned with the same poison that Alex had in his body.'

'What?' cried Liza. 'Is he OK?'

'He's sick,' replied the inspector. 'But he isn't going to die. He didn't drink it, like Alex. He only touched it.'

'Why was *he* touching it?' asked Liza.

'We don't know yet,' said the inspector. 'But Liza, is it possible that Marco got some poison on his hands when he was putting it in Alex's drink? You've already said that Marco was often flirting with Alex. Perhaps he really was very angry about all this?'

'It's not like that at all!' cried Liza. 'Marco was just playing around when he said those things. He just wanted to dance and have a good time last night!'

Liza couldn't understand anything. Her boyfriend and now one of her best friends were both in hospital. She'd been awake all night. And she'd never been more tired in her life. So, when the inspector left to take another phone call, she put her head on the table. She'd always felt so sure about Marco as a good friend – but everything that had once felt clear wasn't now. She remembered a moment just after she and Alex had begun seeing each other. Marco had put out his bottom lip and said: 'I love you, Liza. But I also hate you. Alex was mine and you've broken my heart.'

'Marco,' whispered Liza, falling asleep on the table, 'please say that I didn't break your heart. Please say that you didn't really hate me. And please say that you didn't try to destroy our lives… '

CHAPTER 9
Home again

10.06

Liza slept for an hour before a police officer woke her up. 'The inspector needs to talk to you again,' she said. 'He'll be here in a minute.' Liza sat up in the chair again, still feeling very sleepy.

'Well,' said Inspector Leon, entering the room. 'A lot has happened.'

'Is Alex alive?' asked Liza. 'And Marco… ?'

'Alex is very lucky. Because he's young and strong, he's alive, but he's very ill. Marco is still in hospital too, but he's much better. And we're questioning someone for attempted murder. You're free to go home now, but we may need to bring you back to the police station to answer more questions later.'

'Who?' cried Liza. 'Who are you questioning?'

'I can't tell you that,' the inspector said. 'But you can go home. I'll give you my number. Please call me if you think of anything that we need to know.'

10.43

Liza left through the back door of the police station and found her Aunt Evelyn and Suki waiting for her. They put their arms around her, and held her quietly for a moment. Liza started to feel calm for the first time since the poisoning.

'Can you believe it? They're questioning Veda!' said Suki.

'What?' cried Liza. 'Are you serious?'

'Yes!' said Suki. 'Someone from school saw the police arrive at her house and take her away.'

Veda? Veda had no interest in anyone's boyfriends or girlfriends; she only cared about school. She hadn't liked losing the science award to Liza. But had that really made her poison Liza's boyfriend? That wasn't the Veda Liza knew.

'Have the police made another mistake?' said Liza. 'I mean, a few hours ago, they thought it was Marco. And before that, they thought it was me.'

'Never mind all this right now,' said Evelyn. 'Let's get you home for some food and rest. This has been so awful for you.'

'Have the police made another mistake?' said Liza.

'Can we go to the hospital first? I really want to see Alex – and Marco,' asked Liza.

'Not yet, Liza,' said Evelyn. 'Poor Alex is too sick to see anyone right now.'

'But Marco will come home today,' said Suki. 'Then he'll tell us more.'

Back at the flat, Evelyn brought out a large pot of coffee. Then she started making lunch for them all. Suki's phone had rung just as they'd got back, and she'd stayed outside to take the call. She came and sat down next to Liza, shaking her head.

'So, that was Marco,' she said. 'He's OK. They're just keeping him in the hospital at the moment, but they say if he's still fine by this evening, he can go home tomorrow. The police are questioning Veda because of things that Marco told them.'

'Marco? What things?' asked Liza.

'You probably didn't know that Veda left the dance early – before Alex collapsed and the paramedics and police arrived,' explained Suki. 'Veda was a bit moody – she said that she'd been tired from studying, and she wasn't interested in dancing. You know Veda – nothing is more important than school.'

'Well, yes,' said Liza. 'That's why this is so strange!'

'We were all so upset when the police took you away. Of course, we knew that you hadn't poisoned Alex, and Marco was trying to remember where your bag had been all evening. He asked us all: had anyone taken it from our table, or come and sat in your chair? He wanted to find out what had happened. Veda hadn't danced much all evening, so she'd been at the table more than any of us. Marco decided to go and talk to her on his way home. Ask her some questions.'

'He went to Veda's house?'

'Yes,' said Suki. 'She was asleep, but he phoned her when he was outside her house, and she came down to talk to him. She took him into the kitchen, and he told her everything that had happened at the dance. Veda's parents heard them and woke up, so Veda went to speak to them, while Marco stayed in the kitchen. He moved Veda's coat, which was on a chair, so he could sit down. And as he moved it, a small bottle fell out of the pocket. It was almost empty, but when

When Marco picked the bottle up, his fingers started to hurt.

he picked it up, his fingers started to hurt – and soon they were red and burning.'

'So, he knew it was more of that poison!' cried Liza.

'Yes. But he didn't want Veda to know that he knew, so he put the bottle back into Veda's coat pocket and went to find her. He told her he'd had a phone call from the police and they wanted to ask him some more questions, so he had to go. Then he took a taxi to the police station. But on the way, he began to feel very sick, and the taxi driver took him to the nearest hospital. Marco said he thought he was going to die.'

'This is crazy,' said Liza. 'I just don't understand it.'

She thought for a moment. 'Suki, do you think those anonymous messages came from Veda, too?'

'I do,' said Suki. 'With you in prison, she perhaps hoped to get that science award. And be top of the class again. If you think about it, her parents must have all kinds of things at their lab. Marco said he thinks she probably got the poison there.'

'Veda… a criminal,' said Liza. 'It's hard to believe, isn't it?'

'It is!' said Suki, taking a drink of coffee. 'And now she's going to prison for poisoning your sweet Romeo – but you, Juliet, are free!'

CHAPTER 10
'Can u talk?'

Liza couldn't think about anything for the rest of the day. After Suki had gone, she had a long, hot bath, then she stayed in the flat and tried not to look at her phone. She didn't want to know what everyone was saying about the poisoning. She slept for twelve hours, and when she woke up, the flat was quiet.

For a moment, Liza just enjoyed being in her own bed, warm and comfortable. But when she opened her eyes, she saw Jade's red dress, lying across a chair, and she remembered everything. There was a note by her bed from Evelyn: 'Gone to work, but I can come home if you need me to be there.'

Liza picked up her phone and quickly read the messages that she'd got while she was asleep. Jade had sent the first one: 'ur boyfriend going to live... so happy!' There was also a message from Marco: 'home again, but smokey-eye looking bad. i saved you from prison... you're paying for juan. #makeupmedicine.'

For the first time in many hours, Liza laughed aloud. And it felt really good to laugh. Then she saw something that she hadn't noticed earlier: one of the new messages was anonymous. She felt sick as she opened it. 'can u talk?' it read.

'who is this?' Liza wrote, her hands shaking a little.

'yang,' read the reply. 'must talk'.

But was it really Yang? Liza didn't reply to the anonymous message, but she called Yang on his number.

'Hello, Liza,' he said, answering her call immediately.

'Yang,' said Liza. 'Why are you messaging me anonymously? After everything that's happened? You frightened me!'

'Sorry,' said Yang, keeping his voice very quiet. 'I have a secret, and I don't want any trouble.'

'What secret?' asked Liza, her heart beating faster. Yang didn't answer. 'You're worrying me, Yang. What's wrong with you? OK, I don't like this… I have to go… '

'No!' whispered Yang. 'Don't go, please. It's those anonymous messages that you were getting. I sent them. And I'm so sorry. But I can explain. I love you – and I've always loved you. I never wanted to hurt you; I was just so jealous.'

'I'm calling the police,' said Liza.

'Don't do that,' said Yang. 'Just wait. I'm coming to your flat. I know where you live.'

'No, you don't!' Liza shouted.

'Yes, I do. I'm leaving now.'

Without another word, Liza ended the call. She rang the number that Inspector Leon had given her, and was surprised when he answered at once.

'Yang, the kid I told you about from school – he's coming to my flat right now!' she cried. 'He's just told me that he was the one who was sending the anonymous messages! He sent me another one this morning – and now he wants to talk. He sounded upset… and I don't know what he'll do to me. I'm frightened, really frightened. Inspector, I think you've got the wrong person. I think it's Yang that you want.'

'I'll come with some officers to your home now,' said Inspector Leon. 'Stay on the line and an officer will talk to you while we're on our way. And don't open your door!'

Fifteen minutes later, Inspector Leon and four police officers appeared at Liza's flat in Eastside. Five minutes after that, Yang arrived. The inspector opened the door, and two of the officers immediately took Yang's arms and brought him into the flat.

'Please let me talk!' cried Yang. 'I didn't poison anyone!'

'But you've been sending Liza all those messages – death threats – haven't you?' said the inspector.

'No!' said Yang. 'I never sent her any death threats, I promise. I sent her the first ones, but not those frightening ones. Mine were all stupid little messages. I wanted Liza to think Alex wasn't right for her. And I'm sorry. I'm so sorry. I know it was a horrible thing to do. But I can tell you who wrote the others… and poisoned Alex.'

'Go on,' said the inspector.

'It was Jade,' answered Yang, tears in his eyes. 'I knew it was. But I've been working all night looking for evidence.'

The inspector looked at Yang. 'It's OK,' he said to his officers, and they let Yang go. 'Sit here,' he said, pulling a chair out for him. 'Tell us what you know.'

'Well, a few months ago, Jade had wanted some help from a computer genius, so I'd taught her a few things. One of those things was how to get onto the dark web. And one of them was anonymous messaging. She didn't tell me what it was for, and I didn't ask, because she was paying me a lot of money for the lessons,' Yang added.

'I never sent Liza any death threats, I promise,' said Yang.

'But after Liza showed me those death threats she was getting, I started to feel worried. You see, Jade had asked me how safe anonymous messaging was – if the police saw things you'd written. And I told her that burner phones were safer. I – I just thought perhaps she was selling things. You know. But when I saw that Liza's messages were coming from burner phones, I immediately thought of Jade, so after what happened yesterday, I hacked into her computer and discovered something: she's been on the dark web. Buying poison.'

'Poison,' said Inspector Leon. 'You're sure about this?'

'Really sure,' said Yang, and he took his computer from his bag. 'I've got all the evidence here.'

'OK,' said Inspector Leon. 'I'll need you to come with us to the police station, Yang.' Then he sent three more officers to bring Jade to the station. 'I want her phone and computer – and yours too, Yang. It's going to be another long night.'

◻

'There are two things I still don't understand,' said Marco. The hospital had sent him home later that afternoon, and Liza and Suki had gone to his flat to see him. Marco was lying on his bed, and while the three of them talked about everything that had happened, he ate the chocolates that they'd brought him, one after the other. 'Why did Jade put that second bottle of poison in Veda's coat pocket? Did she actually want everyone to think Veda *and* Liza had poisoned Alex?'

'I know the answer to that,' said Liza. 'Veda and I have the same coat, and when the police gave mine back to me, there was a bill from a restaurant in Northfields in the pocket. I haven't been to Northfields for years – but then I remembered that it's where Veda's grandparents live.'

'So, Jade put the bottle in your coat pocket, but Veda took the wrong coat when she left the party!' said Suki.

'OK, I've got that,' said Marco. 'But why were there two bottles of poison? Jade only needed one, didn't she?'

'Yes, but put yourself in Jade's shoes,' said Suki. 'With only one bottle, she has to find a good time to put the poison in Alex's drink, and then find a good time to put the almost-empty bottle in Liza's bag. It was probably much easier for her just to put the bottle in the bag when she got the chance. I thought of another thing, too,' Suki went on. 'Do you remember that Jade was wearing those purple gloves at the dance? She probably wore them because they stopped her getting ill from touching the poison.'

'Listen to you, girl!' said Marco. 'The way you understand the brain of a criminal makes me worry for you!'

Liza laughed, and then her face looked more serious again as she remembered something. 'You know that Jade sent me one last message, from another phone number?' she said. She opened a message on her phone and showed it to Marco and Suki.

'Never wanted to kill Alex. But I did want to put YOU in prison. He was falling in love with me before you came to Pinewood. Why didn't you stay at a school in Eastside where you belong? And why don't you go back there now!'

'Look at that!' said Suki. 'Do you think that she sent it when she heard the police outside her house?'

'And then threw the phone away,' said Liza. 'Yang said she probably had fifty or sixty burner phones. She sent me one message from each one. He thinks they're probably all at the bottom of the Pinewood River.'

CHAPTER 11

The end?

It was almost the end of the school year at Pinewood Academy. The last month or two had been difficult for everyone, but things were calmer now. And today, Alex had been well enough to return to school.

'Well, I never thought I'd be so happy to be back here at Pinewood Academy,' he said, smiling and standing with Liza and their group of friends. 'Believe me: drinking poison is really not a lot of fun – at the dance or at any other time.'

'Although you weren't my favourite person, Romeo,' said Suki, putting a hand on Alex's shoulder, 'I'm very happy that you're not dead. Welcome back!'

'Thanks, Suki,' replied Alex, smiling. 'I'm happy to be here, too.'

'We're all happy to have you back,' added Veda. 'I'm sure Jade is happy that you're back, too. That means less time in prison for her.'

'Because it's attempted murder and not murder, you mean?' said Yang. 'I don't think someone like Jade will be in prison for long.'

'Probably not,' agreed Alex. 'She has excellent lawyers. They're trying to call it a terrible mistake instead of attempted murder.'

'Well, I hope they don't succeed,' said Veda. 'I still can't believe what she did!'

'Yes, but I think Jade had been in love with Alex all her life,' said Suki. 'When she saw Alex and Liza together, she hated it. And it made her hate Alex as well as Liza. With Liza, he'd found the true love that Jade wanted him to have for her.'

Alex and Liza looked at each other and smiled. Then Alex turned to Yang. 'So Yang, Liza told me you're not in any trouble with the police for your adventures on the dark web and for hacking into other people's computers!'

Yang smiled. 'No, I got a warning, that's all. But I'm not doing anything like that again.'

'Well, thanks for finding the evidence and giving it to the police,' said Alex. 'And thank you, Marco, for... '

'Don't thank Marco for anything!' said Veda, laughing. 'He reported me to the police. Sure, I was upset about the science award, but I don't usually try to kill people for things like that.' The others laughed, too.

'I only hope you're really OK, Alex,' said Marco. 'Just touching and smelling that poison nearly killed me. You're clearly very strong,' he added, feeling Alex's arm.

'Let's not talk about this any more,' said Veda. 'It's all behind us now. I have some great news – I'm going to a science summer school at Harvard in the US this summer. Sorry to say, Liza, but it's the best one in the world – better than the one at Oxford.'

'Well done, Veda!' said Liza happily. 'That's awesome – I can't wait to hear all about it.'

'Thanks,' said Veda proudly. 'They only take three people every year, so I'm really pleased. It isn't free like the one that you won, Liza. But Mum and Dad have enough money to pay for it. Did I ever tell you that my parents are

'It's all behind us now,' said Veda.

successful scientists? And did I tell you that their money built the science lab at the university... and their names are on a building at the hospital?'

'Yes, we all know that,' said Suki. 'You've told us many, many times. And did I ever tell you that my parents work in a restaurant? And did Liza ever tell you that her aunt is a nurse? And did Marco ever tell you that his dad... '

'... is a great man?' said Marco, 'and loves me a lot? So, let's stop this stupid competition. Be happy, Veda. And go to Harvard. But stop talking about it... or... '

'Or what?' asked Veda. 'You'll poison me?'

'Of course not,' answered Marco. 'You need to be alive to take me to the spa on your birthday next week. I nearly died a month ago. A soft, pink robe and some cucumbers over my eyes will help, I'm sure.'

'I think we also need to do something for Yang,' said Suki. 'Perhaps he needs a day at the spa, too.'

'No, thanks,' said Yang quietly. 'Don't spend your money on me. And a day at the spa is not the kind of help that I need.'

'But it is!' Marco cried. 'You have problems, Yang!' he said. 'Under this frightening hair, there's a handsome boy.'

'Do you really think so?' asked Yang, seriously.

'Yes!' said Marco. 'If not the spa, then let's call Jade's friends – Sara for your hair and Juan for your make-up.'

'I don't wear make-up,' said Yang. 'It isn't my thing.'

'Just Sara then, although Juan is wonderful and can teach you a lot about... this,' Marco said, moving his finger in a circle in front of Yang's face. 'You need help... a few skin products, for example.'

'I agree,' said Suki, smiling at Yang. 'You don't want to send sad, broken heart messages anonymously until you're thirty. You're not bad at all, Yang,' she said, putting a hand on his back and then keeping it there. 'In fact, you look really nice behind the… '

'… behind the awful hair,' agreed Marco. 'You'll thank me, Yang. And when Sara has finished, we can buy you some new clothes – with your money from Jade.'

'Great,' said Yang. 'And you can get some new glasses, instead of those strange ones that you wear.'

'Stay in your lane, Yang,' Marco laughed. Then he looked down at his phone, and his smile suddenly disappeared. 'Not another one,' he said. 'Has one of you just sent this? Is this you, Yang? Are you sending anonymous messages again? After everything that's happened to us, this isn't funny.'

'It's not me!' cried Yang. 'I don't do that any more.'

'What is it?' asked Liza, moving next to Marco and reading his message. 'No, that isn't funny at all,' she said, the blood leaving her face.

'What isn't?' asked Suki.

'It's a GIF of a skull laughing,' Liza said. 'And the message says, "this isn't finished…".'

academy *(n)*   a school or place where people study

anonymous *(adj)*   if something is anonymous, you do not know who did, wrote, gave, or made it; **anonymously** *(adv)*

attempt *(v)*   to try to do something; **attempted** *(adj)*

award *(n)*   something valuable or important that you give to somebody who has done something special

awesome *(adj)*   very good, fantastic

believe *(v)*   to feel sure that something is true

block *(v)*   to stop a person or phone number from sending you a message

brain *(n)*   the part inside the head of a person or an animal that thinks and feels

collapse *(v)*   to fall down suddenly

compete *(v)*; **competition** *(n)*   to try to win a race or a competition; a game etc. that people try to win

cucumber *(n)*   a long vegetable with a green skin that is often eaten in salads

dark web *(n)*   people can use a computer to do or buy things here which are against the law

death threat *(n)*   a promise that you will kill someone who does not do what you want

emoji *(n)*   a small picture you can send on a phone or computer that shows what you are feeling or thinking

evidence *(n)*   things that you find or see, which help you to know that something is true

fabulous *(adj)*   something which is very good or wonderful

flirt *(v; n)*   to behave as if you like somebody a lot; a person who behaves as if they like somebody or lots of people; **flirty** *(adj)*

genius *(n)*   a very clever person

GIF *(n)*   a small moving picture or video you can send on a phone or computer to share an idea

glove *(n)* a thing that you wear on your hand

hack *(v)* to use a computer to get into somebody else's computer in order to damage it or get secret information

handsome *(adj)* good-looking

horrible *(adj)* very bad, not nice

jealous *(adj)* angry or sad because you want what another person has; **jealousy** *(n)*

kid *(n)* a young person or child

kiss *(v)* to touch somebody with your lips to show love

laboratory; lab *(n)* a room or building where scientists work

lane *(n)* a narrow road or part of a road

lawyer *(n)* a lawyer knows about law: rules for what people can or cannot do in a country

limo *(n)*; **limousine** *(n)* a big car, which is very comfortable and expensive

make-up *(n)* things like lipstick or powder that you put on your eyes, face, or mouth to change how you look

mean *(adj)* unkind or unpleasant

monster *(n)* a person who does or says very unkind and unpleasant things; an animal in stories that is big and frightening

moody *(adj)* if a person is moody, they aren't happy, and they do or say mean things

paramedic *(n)* a person who is not a doctor or a nurse, but who is able to look after people who are hurt or very ill until they get to hospital

poison *(n; v)* something that will kill you or make you very ill if you eat or drink it; to give a person something that will kill them or make them very ill

product *(n)* something that people use on their hair or skin to make it look better

proud *(adj)* when you have something or do something and are pleased with it; **proudly** *(adv)*

relax *(v)* to rest and be calm; **relaxed** *(adj)*

robe *(n)* a long, soft piece of clothing that a person wears on their body

scholarship *(n)* money that is given to a good student to help them continue studying

science *(n)*; **scientist** *(n)* the study of the natural world; a person who studies science or works with science

spa *(n)* a place where people can go to relax so they look and feel better

tear *(n)* a drop of water that comes from your eye when you cry

trust *(v)* to believe that somebody is honest and good and will not hurt you in any way

upset *(adj)* feeling unhappy or worried

Poisonous

ACTIVITIES

The world of communication

Like most young people around the world, the young people in this story use their phones to communicate with each other. To do this, they can use social media, where people use websites and apps to send messages and information. Some people use social media to send messages, GIFs, and photos to friends and family, while others use it to show photos, videos, and ideas to a large number of people at the same time.

So, when did social media become so popular, and how many users are there across the world today?

In 2004, the social media site MySpace was the first to reach one million monthly users. There had been websites like MySpace before, but it was the first website where users could communicate with so many other people. The social media that we know today started with MySpace.

Since then, many new websites and apps have appeared, and the number of people using them has grown quickly – by the middle of 2022, there were 4.7 billion social media users. That was about 60% of the people in the world!

The use of social media has changed the way that we communicate. We are now able to send messages quickly, easily, and cheaply to a large number of people, anywhere in the world. So social media clearly has many advantages, but, as we see in this story, there are disadvantages, too.

When people meet or speak in real life, they are usually kind and say nice things to each other. But some people are different online and they say mean and upsetting things to other people. Also, because people can be anonymous online, they can send unkind messages without getting in trouble. This has become a really big problem. In 2020, 44% of internet users in the USA had got upsetting messages from other people. Social media is an important part of modern life, but we all need to learn how to use it without hurting other people.

READ & DISCUSS Read 'Beyond the Story' and discuss the answers to these questions.

1 Why do people use social media?

2 What are the advantages of social media?

3 Can you think of more advantages and disadvantages?

4 What research has been done into the disadvantages? What can we do to end these disadvantages?

advantage / disadvantage *(n)* something that helps (doesn't help) or is useful (not useful)

communicate *(v)* to give information or ideas to another person

Think Ahead

1 Read about the story on the back cover. How much do you know about the story? Tick (✓) the true sentences.

   1 Liza is a scholarship student at Pinewood Academy. ☐

   2 Some kids at school aren't friendly to the scholarship students. ☐

   3 Alex doesn't have many friends at Pinewood. ☐

   4 Somebody poisons Liza's boyfriend Alex. ☐

   5 Alex is ill but he doesn't need to go to hospital. ☐

   6 The police ask Liza questions about the poisoning. ☐

2 What do you think is going to happen at the end of the story? Choose one answer.

   1 Alex dies and the police think that Liza murdered him.

   2 Alex doesn't die, but the police think that Liza tried to murder him.

   3 Alex dies and the police think that a Pinewood student murdered him.

   4 Alex doesn't die, but the police think that a Pinewood student tried to murder him.

3 **RESEARCH** Before you read, find the answers to these questions.

   1 Are there schools in your country that students pay a lot of money to go to?

   2 Can students without a lot of money get scholarships to go to these schools? If the answer is yes, how do they get the scholarships?

Chapter Check

CHAPTER 1 Are the sentences true or false?

1 Liza was seventeen years old and Marco and Suki were her friends.

2 Liza was in a police station talking to Inspector Leon.

3 The night before, Liza had collapsed on the dance floor at the school dance.

4 The police had found a bottle of poison in Liza's bag.

5 Someone had sent Liza frightening messages on her phone.

6 Liza lived with her aunt in an expensive part of town.

7 Jade, Yang, Veda, and Alex were scholarship students at Pinewood Academy.

CHAPTER 2 Put the events in order.

a Liza, Alex, Jade, Marco, and Veda went to the school dance in a limo.

b Paramedics and the police arrived at the dance.

c Liza borrowed a red dress from Jade for the school dance.

d Alex met Liza at Jade's house.

e Alex was taken to hospital in an ambulance.

f Liza and Alex danced together on the dance floor.

g The police checked everyone's bags and pockets.

CHAPTER 3 Complete the sentences with the correct words.

computer　friends　messages　scientists　students

1 Suki didn't like the rich _____ at Pinewood Academy.

2 Veda's parents were successful _____.

3 Yang was nice and very good at _____ science.

4 Jade and Alex had been _____ for many years.

5 Liza started getting anonymous _____ on her phone.

CHAPTER 4 Choose the correct words to complete the sentences.

1 Somebody sent Liza a message, but she didn't *understand / read* it.

2 Liza won an important *English / science* award.

3 Alex was very *pleased about / jealous of* Liza's award.

4 *Yang / Veda* won second place in the competition.

5 A few days after the award, *Alex / Yang* became Liza's boyfriend.

CHAPTER 5 Correct the underlined words.

1 The messages Liza got became much <u>better</u> after February.

2 Suki <u>liked</u> Liza and Alex being together.

3 Marco wanted <u>Yang</u> to be his boyfriend.

4 Jade had her make-up done when she wanted to feel <u>sad</u>.

5 Every message to Liza started coming from <u>the same</u> number.

CHAPTER 6 Who says this? Choose the correct person. You will need to use one name twice.

Jade   Liza   Marco   Yang

1 'Someone wants to kill me.'

2 'The messages are coming from burner phones.'

3 'You and I are going to a spa.'

4 'I want to relax and be happy! Who's paying?'

5 'You aren't Alex's first love, and you won't be his last.'

CHAPTER 7 Tick (✓) the true sentences.

1 Jade took some money from Liza for the spa. ☐

2 After the spa, Liza and the others saw Suki with Veda and Yang. ☐

3 Alex was at a business lunch with his parents on the day Liza went to the spa. ☐

4 Liza called Alex, but he didn't answer. ☐

5 After she spoke to Alex, Liza got three frightening messages on her phone. ☐

CHAPTER 8 Choose the correct answers.

1 Alex started to get…

   a anonymous messages.

   b messages that said he was going to die.

2 The inspector said that all Liza's friends…

   a had a reason to make trouble for her and Alex.

   b had sent her frightening messages.

3 Marco had…

   a drunk the poison.

   b touched the poison.

CHAPTER 9 Complete the sentences with the names of people in the story. You will need to use one name twice.

Liza   Marco   Suki   Veda

1 When _____ left the police station, she saw her Aunt Evelyn and Suki.

2 Liza was surprised when she heard that the police were questioning _____.

3 _____ had found some poison in Veda's coat pocket.

4 _____ thought that it was Veda who had sent the anonymous messages.

5 Marco thought that _____ got the poison from her parents' lab.

CHAPTER 10 Answer the questions.

1 Who sent the first anonymous messages to Liza?

2 Who sent the death threats to Liza?

3 Who found evidence that Jade had poisoned Alex?

4 What did Jade buy on the dark web?

5 Whose coat did Veda take when she left the party?

CHAPTER 11 Choose the correct words.

1 After many *days / weeks*, Alex returned to Pinewood.

2 Suki was *happy / unhappy* to see Alex back at school.

3 Yang *spent time in prison / got a warning* for going on the dark web and hacking into people's computers.

4 *Yang / Someone* sent Marco a message saying 'this isn't finished'.

Focus on Vocabulary

1 **Complete the sentences with the correct words.**

anonymous   evidence   proud   scholarship

1 The messages were _____ so Liza didn't know who had sent them.

2 Aunt Evelyn was very _____ of Liza because she worked hard and was successful at school.

3 Yang found _____ to show that Jade had bought the poison on the dark web.

4 Students without a lot of money can get a _____ to help them pay for Pinewood Academy.

2 **Read the clues and complete the word puzzle.**

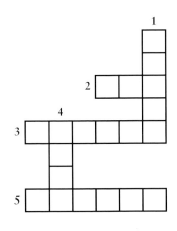

Down

1 water that comes from your eyes when you cry

4 a long and expensive car

Across

2 a place where you go to relax

3 you wear these on your hands

5 something that can make you sick, or kill you if you eat or drink it

Focus on Language

1 Complete the sentences using the past perfect form of the verbs in brackets.

*Liza was at the police station because a police officer <u>had found</u> (**find**) a bottle of poison in her bag.*

1 Liza was warm because a police officer _____ (**give**) her a blanket.

2 Alex _____ (**be**) really happy before he collapsed on the dance floor.

3 The girls laughed at Liza because they _____ (**see**) her getting on a bus to Eastside.

4 Liza was pleased because she _____ (**make**) some good friends at Pinewood Academy.

2 DECODE Read the extract and <u>underline</u> the contractions.

Suki took Liza's hand and smiled. 'OK, I'm sorry,' she said. 'And I'm sure it isn't fun to get all this rubbish on your phone… but it is strange to see you and Alex together. I didn't think you'd fall in love with a rich, Pinewood boy – a person who doesn't have to work for a thing and just goes into business with Mummy and Daddy. I thought that you'd like someone more interesting.'

3 DECODE Look at the contractions that end in *'d*. Answer the questions.

1 What word does the *'d* stand for?

2 Suki is using reported speech to tell Liza about her thoughts. Rewrite the sentences in direct speech.

Discussion

1 **Complete the advice with the words below.**

idea important mustn't should shouldn't

1 If you get anonymous or frightening messages, you _____ always tell an adult that you trust.

2 You _____ share personal information like your address or phone number online.

3 You _____ send frightening, upsetting, or mean messages to anyone.

4 If you are worried about something you see online, it's _____ to tell someone about it.

5 It isn't a good _____ to talk to strangers online.

2 **THINK CRITICALLY** Do you agree with the advice in exercise 1? Why / Why not?

3 **Match the Pinewood students with their problems.**

1 Marco…   a is jealous of Liza's science award.

2 Veda…   b hates the rich Pinewood students.

3 Yang…   c likes Liza's boyfriend.

4 Suki…   d is in love with Liza.

4 **COMMUNICATE** Think about the Pinewood students in exercise 3 and their problems. Talk to your partner about the advice you would give them. Use some of the phrases in exercise 1.

1 Read Liza's social media profile.

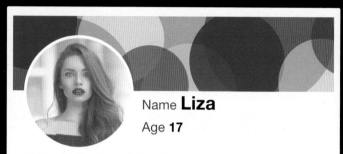

Name **Liza**

Age **17**

School **Pinewood Academy**

Likes **Good friends, pizza, and cats**

Dislikes **Mean friends!**

Hi, I'm Liza, and I'm a scholarship student at Pinewood Academy. Yes, that's right – I said a scholarship student! I'm not from the nice side of town. I don't live in a big house with a pool, and I don't get driven to school every day in a fabulous car. I'm from Eastside. I live in a small flat, and I catch the bus there every day after school.

I live with my Aunt Evelyn. Evelyn's a nurse and she works really hard to help me at school and to buy me the things I need. She was so proud of me when I got my scholarship to Pinewood. She thinks that I'm going to become a successful scientist one day. I hope she's right because that's my dream, too!

2 Read Liza's profile again and write questions for these answers.

1 good friends, pizza, and cats

2 mean friends

3 in a small flat in Eastside

4 on the bus

5 with her Aunt Evelyn

6 a scientist

3 **COLLABORATE** Work with a partner. Talk about one of the other Pinewood students. What answers would they give to the questions in exercise 2? Use information from the story and your own ideas.

4 **CREATE** Imagine that you are the Pinewood student you and your partner talked about in Collaborate. Write your social media profile.

5 **COMMUNICATE** Work in groups. Look at all the social media profiles and discuss them. Vote for the most interesting profile.

If you liked this Bookworm, why not try...

Justice

LEVEL 3
Tim Vicary

London: November. Terrorists blow up the Queen's coach outside Parliament. The Queen escapes, but five people are killed, and 40 others badly hurt – ordinary, innocent people like Alan Cole, the Queen's coachman. And for Alan's daughter Jane, there is more terror to come, in the search for the truth behind the bombing. Will the terrorists be caught and brought to justice?

Love Story

LEVEL 3
Erich Segal

This is a love story you won't forget. Oliver Barrett meets Jenny Cavilleri. He plays sports. She plays music. He's rich, and she's poor. They argue, and they fight, and they fall in love.

So, they get married, and make a home together. They work hard, they enjoy life, they make plans for the future. Then they learn they don't have much time left.
